Measurement Day

One morning, Anya looks around for something to play with.

She spots an interesting object in a basket of toys.

"What's this, Mama?" she asks.

"That's a tape measure. It's a tool that tells you how long, tall, or wide things are."

"Today," Anya announces grandly, "is Measurement Day."

"How fun! Make sure to include your little brother," says Mama.

"Can I have it?" her brother Kavi asks.

"You can watch me," says Anya.

They head outside.

Anya measures how long her arms are, stretching them out as wide as they can go. "43 inches long!"

"That's called your wingspan," Papa says.

"What's my wingspan?" Kavi asks, and starts flapping his arms around.

"I'm taller than you, Kavi," Anya says.

"Look, I'm as TALL as this tree. You only come up to that short little bush."

Kavi stomps his feet.

"Watch, I can jump farther."
Anya jumps with both feet and
measures the length of her jump.

"38 inches!" she says.

Kavi jumps, too. "I jumped
1,000 inches!"

"No, you didn't," says Anya. "Your
jump is shorter."

"When is it going to be my turn?"
Kavi asks.

"Anya, let Kavi try it," Mama says.

Anya drops the tape measure on
the ground.

"Hey! That's not nice!" Kavi says.

Kavi measures Mama's leg.
"One million inches high!" he says.

"That's not right," Anya says.
"It's 36 inches. That's three feet."

"One million," Kavi repeats.

"You can measure around things, too," Papa says. "I'll wrap the tape measure around Kavi's head. Let's see... almost two feet around. That's a good-sized noggin!"

"My head is BIGGER," Anya says. "And so are my feet."

"It looks like you're having a hard
 time sharing and being kind today,"
 Mama says.

"I'm mad!" says Kavi.

"I'm frustrated!" says Anya.

"What do you need to say to each other?" asks Mama.

Kavi looks at Anya. "I don't like that you keep saying you're BIGGER and I'm so small."

Next, it's Anya's turn: "I don't like how you keep following me around. I found the measuring tape."

"How can we fix this?" Mama asks.

"I know!" Anya says. "What if we measure things together? I'll hold the tape, and you hold the other end."

Kavi thinks about it. "Okay!"

Anya gives her little brother a big hug. He hugs her back tightly. "Hey, can I measure your hug?" Mama asks.

"Yeah!" both kids say together. Mama wraps the measuring tape around them.

"38 inches," she says. "A lot of love fits into that."